Emmet Fox Explains

Watchmaker Publishing

ISBN 978-1-60386-749-8

Contents

The Hidden Power

trange as it may seem to you, there exists a mystic power that is able to transform your life so thoroughly, so radically, so completely, that when the process is completed your own friends would hardly recognize you, and, in fact, you would scarcely be able to recognize yourself. You would sit down and ask yourself: "Can I really be the man or woman that I vaguely remember, who went about under my name six months or six years ago? Was I really that person? Could that person have possibly been me?" And the truth will be that while in one sense you are indeed the same person, yet in another sense you will be someone utterly different.

This mystic but intensely real force can pick you up today, now, from the midst of failure, ruin, misery, despair – and in the twinkling of an eye, as Paul said, solve your problems, smooth out your difficulties, cut you free from any entanglements, and place you clear, safe, and happy upon the highroad of freedom and opportunity.

It can lift you out of an invalid's bed, make you sound and well once more, and free to go out into the world to shape your life as you will. It can throw open the prison door and liberate the captive. It has a magical healing balm for the bruised or broken heart.

This mystic Power can teach you all things that you need to know, if only you are receptive and teachable. It can inspire you with new thoughts and ideas, so that your work may be truly original. It can impart new and wonderful kinds of knowledge as soon as you really want such knowledge – glorious knowledge – strange things not taught in schools or written in books. It can do for you that which is probably the most important thing of all in your present stage: it can find your true place in life for you, and put you into it too. It can find the right friends for you, kindred spirits who are interested in the same ideas and want the same things that you do. It can provide you with an ideal home. It can furnish you with the prosperity that means freedom, freedom to be and to do and to go as your soul calls.

This extraordinary Power, mystic though I have rightly called it, is nevertheless very real, no mere imaginary abstraction, but actually the most practical thing there is. The existence of this Power is already well known to thousands of people in the world today, and has been known to certain enlightened souls for tens of thousands of years. This Power is really no less than the primal Power of Being, and to discover that Power is the Divine birthright of all men. It is your right and your privilege to make your contact with this Power, and to allow it to work through your body, mind, and estate, so that you need no longer grovel upon the ground amid limitations and difficulties, but can soar up on wings like an eagle to the realm of dominion and joy.

But where, it will naturally be asked, is this wonderful, mystic Power to be contacted? Where may we find it? And how is it brought into action? The answer is perfectly simple – This Power is to be found within your own consciousness, the last place that most people would look for it. Right within your own mentality there lies a source of energy stronger than electricity, more potent than high explosive; unlimited and inexhaustible. You only need to make conscious contact with this Power to set it working in your affairs; and all the marvelous results enumerated can be yours. This is the real meaning of such sayings in the Bible as "The Kingdom of God is within you"; and "Seek ye first the Kingdom of God, and all the rest shall be added."

This Indwelling Power, the Inner Light, or Spiritual Idea, is spoken of in the Bible as a child, and throughout the Scriptures the child symbolically always stands for this. Bible symbolism has its own beautiful logic, and just as the soul is always spoken of as a woman, so this, the Spiritual Idea that is born to the soul, is described as a child.

The conscious discovery by you that you have this Power within you, and your determination to make use of it, is the birth of the child. And it is easy to see how very apt the symbol is, for the infant that is born in consciousness is just such a weak, feeble entity as any new-born child, and it calls for the same careful nursing and guarding that any infant does in its earliest days. After a time, however, as the weeks go by, the child grows stronger and bigger, until a time comes when it can well take care of itself; and then it grows and grows in wisdom and stature until, no longer leaning on the mother's care, the child, now arrived at man's estate, turns the tables, and repays its debt by taking over the care of its mother. So, your ability to contact the mystic Power within yourself, frail and feeble at first, will gradually develop until you find yourself permitting that Power to take your whole life into its care.

The life story of Jesus, the central figure of the Bible, perfectly dramatizes this truth. He is described as being born of a virgin, and in a poor stable, and we know how he grew up to be the Savior of the world. Now, in Bible symbolism, the virgin soul means the soul that looks to God alone, and it is this condition of soul in which the child, or Spiritual Idea, comes to birth. It is when we have reached that stage, the stage where, either through wisdom or because of suffering, we are prepared to put God really first, that the thing happens.

Different People See Different Worlds

What we experience is our own concept of things. That is why no two people see quite the same world, and why, in many cases, different people see such different worlds. To put it in another way, we make our own world by the way in which we think; for we really do live in a world of our own thoughts. It follows from this that if our thinking is faulty, our conditions must be faulty too until our thinking is corrected; and that it is useless to try to improve outer things if we leave our own mentality unchanged.

Let us suppose for the sake of example that a deaf man goes to Carnegie Hall to a Kreisler recital; and that he happens to be a very foolish person. He sits in the middle of the orchestra and, of course, he does not hear a sound. He is annoyed at this, and changes his ticket for a seat in the first balcony. Here, naturally, he fares no better, and, foolishly thinking that the acoustics of the building are at fault, moves again to the top balcony. Still he cannot hear a sound; so now he goes downstairs again and this time chooses a seat in the very front of the orchestra, only a few yards from the violinist.

Of course, he has no better fortune here, and so he stamps out of the theatre in a huff, declaring that evidently Kreisler cannot play, and that the hall is badly designed for music.

It is easy for us to see that the trouble is really within himself, and that he cannot remedy matters by merely changing his seat. The only thing for him to do is to overcome his deafness in some way, and then he will enjoy the concert. He must change himself.

This parable applies literally to all the problems of life. We see inharmony[1] because of a spiritual lack within ourselves. As we gain greater spiritual understanding, the true Nature of Being opens up. As long as we move from one place to another in search of harmony, or try to bring it about by changing outer things, we are like the foolish man who could not hear Kreisler, and ran about all over the theatre.

Free Will *or* Fate

The capriciousness of destiny was a favorite subject with the old-fashioned novelists. In their three-volume world, people's lives were at the mercy of trifling accidents from day to day. A person's whole life was spoilt because one letter was stolen or went astray. The hero

---

[1] Lack of harmony; discord –

rose from obscurity to wealth and fame through meeting a casual stranger in a railroad car, or through saving someone from drowning at the seashore. One false step ruined an otherwise promising career. One turn of fortune's wheel solved all problems for someone else.

All this is nonsense. We are not at the mercy of accidents for there are no accidents, and trifles have only trifling effects. In the long run you demonstrate your character; and you cannot ultimately miss the mark for which you are fitted, because of any outer accident. A particular incident may give you a temporary advantage or cause you passing grief or inconvenience, but it does not change your life's story.

An energetic and enterprising man who attends to his business will make a success of his life whether he meets a helpful stranger in a railroad car or not – and whether a particular letter concerning him is lost or not. The miscarriage of a letter may deprive him of a particular position; meeting with a helpful and influential stranger may bring his success a little sooner; but if he has the qualities demanded for success he will succeed in any case. And if he lacks those qualities no help from the outside can make him successful. No nation is destroyed by the loss of one battle. When a nation is weak in natural resources and divided within itself, it cannot stand; but it is this structural weakness that brings about its fall. If it were united, well organized, and armed, it could lose that battle and still win the war. Your own character makes or breaks you. This is true of the individual, of a nation, of a party, of a church, or of any institution.

If you seem to yourself to be lacking in certain necessary qualities, if your character seems to lack strength, ask God to give you what you need – and He will. You can build any quality into your mentality by meditating upon that quality every day.

Mind Your Own Business

One of the first rules on the spiritual path is that you must attend strictly to your own business and not interfere with that of others. Your neighbor's life is sacred and you have no right to try to manage it for him. Let him alone. God has given him free will and self-determination, so why should you interfere?

Many well-meaning people are constantly "butting-in" to their neighbors' lives without invitation. They pretend to themselves that their only desire is to help, but this is self-deception. It is really a desire to interfere. Interference always does more harm than good. Actually, those who mind other people's business always neglect their own.

The man who wants to put your house in order has always made a failure of his own life. M.Y.O.B.[2] Of course, this does not mean that you are not to help people whenever you can; in fact, you should make it a rule to try to do at least one kind act every day; but you must do it without interfering or encroaching. When in doubt, claim Divine Guidance.

It is always right to give your neighbor the right thought. Under any circumstances it can only do good to "Golden Key" him when you think of him. Don't fuss – God is running the universe.

New Thought

As far as God is concerned, there is no check of any kind upon the amount of divine energy that we can appropriate, or, therefore, upon the things that we can do or be. Yet, for practical purposes, you can draw from the inexhaustible Source only in accordance with the measure of your understanding, just as you can draw water from the Atlantic only in accordance with the size of the vessel that you use. Almost everyone is foolishly content to fill his pitcher, small as

---

[2] Mind your own business -

it may be, to somewhere very short of the top. The true manner of God's working is illustrated by a simple anecdote. A certain man was working in his garden, assisted by his little girl who had undertaken the task of watering the lawn by means of the usual rubber hose. Suddenly she cried out: "Daddy, the water has stopped." The father looked over, and, taking in the situation quietly, said, "Well, take your foot off the hose."

The ultimate cause of all our troubles is just this. Behind all secondary and proximate causes lies the same primary mistake. We have been pressing our feet and the whole weight of our mentality upon the pipe line of life, and then complaining because the water does not flow. *And the Lord shall guide thee continually, and satisfy thy soul in drought... and thou shalt be like a watered garden, and like a spring of water, whose waters fail not.*[3]

Jesus has told us that we always demonstrate our consciousness. We always demonstrate what we habitually have in our mind. What sort of mind have you? Do not let anyone else tell you, because they do not know. People who like you will think your mentality is better than it is; those who do not like you will think it is worse, just examine your conditions and see what you are demonstrating. This method is scientific and infallible. If an automobile engineer is working out a new design for an engine, for instance, he doesn't say: "I wonder what Smith thinks about this. I like Smith. If Smith is against this I won't try it." Nor does he say, "I won't try this idea because it comes from France." He is impersonal and unemotional about it. He says, "I will test it out, and decide by the results I obtain." All that anyone can do for you is to help you change your thought. You yourself must keep it changed. No one else can think for you. "*No man can save his brother's soul or pay his brother's debt.*" *...and I will put a new spirit within you...*[4]

---

[3] *Isaiah 58:11*
[4] *Ezekiel 11:19* -

No Reality *in* Evil

Never recognize evil as having any reality. Never grant it the courtesy of the slightest or most formal acquiescence. Even though you may not be able to demonstrate over error for the time being, still you must not recognize it as having any power or reality.

Every time you speak or think of evil as having any power – you give it that much power. Every time you allow it to scare you – you give it that much authority.

Always fight error in thought – not in the sense of struggling with it, but fight it in the sense of knowing that it is only false belief. Do not let it rest quietly in thought; but harass it.

An old soldier who was with Grant during most of the Civil War, once said; "The difference between Grant and McClellan was this – McClellan was a mighty fine soldier, knew all the military textbooks by heart and what you ought to do – but he wouldn't fight.

When Lincoln would ask him to fight, he would say, 'Not ready yet' or 'We must be thoroughly prepared for a thing like that; next year maybe.' But Grant, he was always fighting. No matter how few men Grant had with him, if the enemy was anywhere near, Grant took a sock at him. Grant would always fight."

The only attitude for the metaphysical student is; "I believe in Divine Harmony and nothing else. I do not believe there is any power in evil, and it is not going to get any recognition from me. The Truth about my problem is true now, not next week or next year but now, and the Truth concerning anything is all that there is of it." This is the scientific way of fighting and harassing error – to see that it has no chance to dig itself in. This is the General Grant touch.

Judge not according to the appearance, but judge righteous judgment.

Prophecy *for* Yourself

Thoughtless people sometimes say that our affirmations and meditations are foolish because we state what is not so. "To claim that my body is well or being healed when it is not, is only to tell a lie," said one distinguished man some years ago.

This is to misunderstand the whole principle. We affirm the harmony that we seek in order to provide the subconscious with a blue print of the work to be done. When you decide to build a house, you purchase a vacant piece of ground and then your architect prepares drawings of a complete house. Actually, of course, there is no such house on the lot today, but you would not think of saying that the architect was drawing a lie. He is drawing what is to be, in order that it may be. So, we build in thought the conditions that will later come into manifestation on the physical plane.

To wait like Mr. Micawber for things to "turn up" is foolish, because you will probably die before they do so. What is your intelligence for if not to be used in building the kind of life that you want? Very primitive men in prehistoric times rejoiced when they found food growing anywhere, and then they waited, perhaps for years, until they happened to find another crop. Today we use our intelligence, and plant in good time the actual crops that we want, and the amount that we consider necessary. We do not sit about hoping that wheat or barley may fortunately come up somewhere. If we did that, civilization would collapse.

The Key *of* Destiny

There are a few great laws that govern all thinking just as there are a few fundamental laws in chemistry, in physics, and in mechanics, for example. We know that thought control is the Key of Destiny, and in order to learn thought control we have to know and understand these laws, just as the chemist has to understand the laws of chemistry, and the electrician has to know the laws of electricity. One of the great mental laws is the Law of Substitution. This means that the only way to get rid of a certain thought is to substitute another one for it. You cannot dismiss a thought directly. You can do so only by substituting another one for it. On the physical plane this is not the case. You can drop a book or a stone by simply opening your hand and letting it go; but with thought this will not work. If you want to dismiss a negative thought, the only way to do so is to think of something positive and constructive. It is as though in order, let us say, to drop a pencil, it were necessary to put a pen or a book or a stone into your hand, when the pencil would fall away.

If I say to you, "Do not think of the Statue of Liberty," of course, you immediately think of it. If you say, "I am not going to think of the Statue of Liberty," that is thinking of it. But now, having thought of it, if you become interested in something else, say, by turning on the radio, you forget all about the Statue of Liberty – and this is a case of substitution.

It sometimes happens that negative thoughts seem to besiege you in such force that you cannot overcome them. That is what is called a fit of depression, or a fit of worry, or perhaps even a fit of anger. In such a case the best thing is to go and find someone to talk to on any subject, or to go to a good movie or play, or read an interesting book, say a good novel or biography or travel book, or something of the kind. If you sit down to fight the negative tide you will probably succeed only in amplifying it.

Turn your attention to something quite different, refusing steadfastly to think of or rehearse the difficulty, and, later on, after you have completely gotten away from it, you can come back with confidence and handle it by spiritual treatment. *I say unto you that you resist not evil.*[5]

Law *of* Circulation

The law of circulation is a Cosmic Law. That means that it is true everywhere and on all planes. The law is that constant rhythmical movement is necessary to health and harmony. Now the

---

[5] *Matthew 5.39*

opposite of circulation is congestion, and it may be said that all sickness, inharmony, or trouble of any kind is really due to some form of congestion.

If you think this subject out for yourself you will be fascinated to find how generally true it is, and in what unexpected places it appears. Much ill health is due to emotional congestion. This leads to congestion of the nerve, blood, and lymphatic fluids, producing disease. The depression belief under which the country labored for ten years was a case of congestion. There was plenty of raw material, machinery, and skill, and a very wide – spread demand for goods; but a case of congestion occurred! The dust bowl trouble and its allied misfortune, the floods, is, of course, an example of congestion. War itself is really due to frustrated circulation on many planes of existence.

Some students of metaphysics shut their minds to the reception of new truth, and this always produces mental congestion and a failure to demonstrate. You should treat yourself two or three times a week for free circulation on all planes – by claiming that God is bringing this about.

What *is* Your Because?

When you find yourself thinking that your prayer cannot be answered for any reason – treat that reason. When something says that you cannot demonstrate "because" – treat the because. When you think, I cannot demonstrate because I have not enough understanding, treat for understanding. When you think, I cannot demonstrate because I have a headache – treat the headache. When you think, I cannot demonstrate because I am full of doubts – treat the doubts. When you think, I cannot demonstrate because it is now too late – treat against the time illusion. When you think, I cannot demonstrate because in this part of the country – treat against space illusion. When you think, I cannot demonstrate because of my age – treat your age belief. When you think, I cannot demonstrate because someone else will hinder me – treat the belief in a power other than God. No matter what name the because may give itself, it is still your belief in limitation. Be loyal to God and know that He and He alone has all the power. Treat the because.

Yesterday's Tears

Never tell people about the fine thing you are going to do, but wait until you have done it, and then show them the completed article. Never point to an empty lot and say: "I am going to build a tower there"; but wait until the edifice is complete, and then if you like, say: "Look at the tower I have built." But when the tower is there it will not really be necessary to say anything at all, because it will speak for itself.

Talking about your plans before they have actually materialized, is the surest way to destroy them. It is a universal law of nature that the unborn child is protected from all contact with the world; in fact this is the real function of motherhood. Now the inspiration that comes to you is your child; you are its mother; and nature intends that you should protect and nourish that idea in secrecy and shelter, up to the moment when it is ready to emerge upon the material plane.

To chatter or boast about it is to expose it to the world and kill it. This applies to any new enterprise that you may be contemplating, as well as to a new idea. An important business deal, for instance, a large sale, the buying of a house, the forming of a partnership, should be protected in the same way. Don't discuss these things at the luncheon table, or anywhere else.

Keep your business to yourself. Of course, it is quite permissible to consult experts, and to reveal your plan where it is absolutely necessary to do so. This is nourishing the idea, not exposing It. It is chatter, gossip, and boasting that are to be avoided. In quietness and confidence shall be your strength.

How *to* Get *a* Demonstration

Here is one way of solving a problem by Scientific by Scientific Prayer, or, as we say in metaphysics, of getting a demonstration.

Get by yourself, and be quiet for a few moments. This is very important. Do not strain to think rightly or to find the right thought, etc., but just be quiet. Remind yourself that the Bible says Be still, and know that I am God.

Then begin to think about God. Remind yourself of some of the things that you know about Him – that He is present everywhere, that He has all power, that He knows you and loves you and cares for you, and so forth. Read a few verses of the Bible, or a paragraph from any spiritual book that helps you.

During this stage it is important not to think about your problem, but to give your attention to God. In other words, do not try to solve your problem directly (which would be using will power) but rather become interested in thinking of the Nature of God.

Then claim the thing that you need – a healing, or some particular good which you lack. Claim it quietly and confidently; as you would ask for something to which you are entitled.

Then give thanks for the accomplished fact; as you would if somebody handed you a gift. Jesus said when you pray believe that you receive and you shall receive.

Do not discuss your treatment (prayer) with anyone.

Try not to be tense or hurried. Tension and hurry delay the demonstration. You know that if you try to unlock a door hurriedly, the key is apt to stick, whereas, if you do it slowly, it seldom does. If the key sticks, the thing is to stop pressing, take your breath, and release it gently. To push hard with will power can only jam the lock completely. So, it is with mental working.

In quietness and confidence shall be your strength.

The Presence

God is the only Presence and the only Power. God is fully present here with me, now. God is the only real Presence – all the rest is but shadow. God is perfect Good, and God is the cause only of perfect Good. God never sends sickness, trouble, accident, temptation, nor death itself; nor does He authorize these things. We bring them upon ourselves by our own wrong thinking. God, Good, can cause only good. The same fountain cannot send forth both sweet and bitter water.

I am Divine Spirit. I am the child of God. In God I live and move and have my being; so I have not fear. I am surrounded by the Peace of God and all is well. I am not afraid of people; I am not afraid of things; I am not afraid of circumstances; I am not afraid of myself; for God is with me. The Peace of God fills my soul, and I have no fear. I dwell in the Presence of God, and no fear can touch me. I am not afraid of the past; I am not afraid of the present; I am not afraid for the future; for God is with me. The Eternal God is my dwelling place and underneath are the ever-lasting arms. Nothing can ever touch me but the direct action of God Himself, and God is Love.

God is Life; I understand that and I express it. God is Truth; I understand that and I express it. God is Divine Love; I understand that and I express it.

I send out thoughts of love and peace and healing to the whole universe: to all trees and plants and growing things, to all beasts and birds and fishes, and to every man, woman and child on earth, without any distinction. If anyone has ever injured me or done me any kind of harm, I fully and freely forgive him now, and the thing is done forever. I loose him and let him go. I am free and he is free. It there is any burden of resentment in me I cast it upon the Christ within, and I go free.

God is Infinite Wisdom, and that Wisdom is mine. That Wisdom leads and guides me; so, I shall not make mistakes. Christ in me is a lamp unto my feet. God is Infinite Life, and that Life is my supply; so I shall want for nothing. God created me and He sustains me. Divine Love has foreseen everything, and provided for everything.

One Mind, One Power, One Principle. One God, One Law, One Element. Closer is He than breathing, nearer than hands and feet.

I am Divine Sprit, the Child of God, and in the presence of God I dwell forever. I thank God for Perfect Harmony.

Cause *and* Effect

Whatever you experience in your life is really but the outpicturing of your own thoughts and beliefs. Now, you can change these thoughts and beliefs, and then the outer picture must change too. The outer picture cannot change until you change your thought. Your real heartfelt conviction is what you outpicture or demonstrate, not your mere pious opinions or formal assents.

Convictions cannot be adopted arbitrarily just because you want a healing. They are built up by the thoughts you think and the feelings you entertain day after day as you go through life. So, it is your habitual mental conduct that weaves the pattern of your destiny for you, and is not this just as it should be?

So, no one else can keep you out of your kingdom – or put you into it either.

The story of your life is really the story of the relations between yourself and God.

Faith

Verily, I say unto you, *If ye have faith, and doubt not, ye shall not only do this which is done to the fig tree, but also if ye shall say unto this mountain, be thou removed, and be thou cast into the sea; it shall be done.*[6]

An understanding faith is the life of prayer. It is a great mistake, however to struggle to produce a lively faith within yourself. That can only end in failure. The thing to do is to act as though you had faith. What we voluntarily do will always be the expression of our

[6]*Matthew 21:21* -

true belief. Act out the part that you wish to demonstrate, and you will be expressing true faith. "Act as though I were, and I will be," says the Bible in effect. This is the right use of the will, scientifically understood.

The statement of Jesus quoted above is perhaps the most tremendous spiritual pronouncement ever made. Probably no other teacher who ever lived would have dared to say it, but Jesus knew the law of faith and proved it himself many times. We shall move mountains when we are willing to believe that we can, and then not only will mountains be moved, but the whole planet will be redeemed and re-formed according to the Pattern in the Mount.

Know the Truth about your problems. Claim spiritual dominion. Avoid tenseness, strain, and over-anxiety. Expect your prayer to be answered, and act as though you expected it.

Flee *to the* Mountains

When ye therefore shall see the abomination of desolation, spoken of by Daniel the prophet, stand in the holy place, (who so readeth, let him understand:) *Then let them which be in Judea flee into the mountains: Let him which is on the housetop not come down to take anything out of his house: Neither let him which is in the field return back to take his clothes.*[7]

The moment you catch yourself thinking a negative thought, you should reject it instantly. Immediately switch your attention to the Presence of God. Do not stop to say "good-bye" to the error thought, but break the connection instantly and occupy your mind with good; you will be surprised how many difficulties will begin to melt away out of your life. Indeed, we may say that when error presents itself to consciousness, the first five seconds are Golden.

In the text quoted above, Jesus teaches this lesson in his own graphic way. The immediate application of these words was, of

---

[7] *Matthew 24:1 5-1 8*

course, to the coming siege of Jerusalem, but the idea involved is eternal. The holy place is your consciousness, and the abomination of desolation is any negative thought, because a negative thought means belief in the absence of God at the point concerned. Those who are in Judea are those who believe that prayer does change things; to flee to the mountains means to pray, especially that quick switching of the thought to the Presence of God, which I have mentioned.

Now You Must Do It

The only part of our religion that is real is the part we express in our daily lives. Ideals that we do not act out in practice are mere abstract theories and have no real meaning. Actually, such pretended ideals are a serious detriment, because they drug the soul into a false sense of security.

If you want to receive any benefit from your religion you must practice it, and the place to practice it is right here where you are, and the time to do it is now.

Divine Love is the only real power. If you can realize this fact even dimly it will begin to heal and harmonize every condition in your life within a few hours. The way to realize this fact is to express it in every word you speak, in every business transaction, in every social activity, and, in fact, in every phase of your life.

An early New Thought writer said: "Knead love into the bread you bake; wrap strength and courage in the parcel you tie for the woman with the weary face; hand trust and candor with the coin you pay to the man with the suspicious eyes." This is beautifully said, and it sums up the Practice of the Presence of God.

Forgiveness

Forgive us our trespasses,
as we forgive them
that trespass against us.

This clause is the turning point of the Prayer. It is the strategic key to the whole Treatment. Let us notice here that Jesus has so arranged this marvelous Prayer that it covers the entire ground of the unfoldment of our souls completely, and in the most concise and telling way. It omits nothing that is essential for our salvation, and yet, so compact is it that there is not a thought or a word too much. Every idea fits into its place with perfect harmony and in perfect sequence. Anything more would be redundance, anything less would be incompleteness, and at this point it takes up the critical factor of forgiveness.

Having told us what God is, what man is, how the universe works, how we are to do our own work – the salvation of humanity and of our own souls – he then explains what our true nourishment or supply is, and the way in which we can obtain it; and now he comes to the forgiveness of sins.

The forgiveness of sins is the central problem of life. Sin is a sense of separation from God, and is the major tragedy of human experience. It is, of course, rooted in selfishness. It is essentially an attempt to gain some supposed good to which we are not entitled in justice. It is a sense of isolated, self-regarding, personal existence, whereas the Truth of Being is that all is One. Our true selves are at one with God, undivided from Him, expressing His ideas, witnessing to His nature – the dynamic Thinking of that Mind. Because we are all one with the great Whole of which we are spiritually a part, it follows that we are one with all men. Just because in Him we live and move and have our being, we are, in the absolute sense, all essentially one.

Evil, sin, the fall of man, in fact, is essentially the attempt to negative this Truth in our thoughts. We try to live apart from God. We try to do without Him. We act as though we had life of our own; as separate minds; as though we could have plans and purposes and interests separate from His. All this, if it were true, would mean that existence is not one and harmonious, but a chaos of competition and strife. It would mean that we are quite separate from our fellow man and could injure him, rob him, or hurt him, or even destroy him, without any damage to ourselves, and, in fact, that the more we took from other people the more we should have for ourselves. It would mean that the more we considered our own interests, and the more indifferent we were to the welfare of others, the better off we should be. Of course, it would then follow naturally that it would pay others to treat us in the same way, and that accordingly we might expect many of them to do so. Now if this were true, it would mean that the whole universe is only a jungle, and that sooner or later it must destroy itself by its own inherent weakness and anarchy. But, of course, it is not true and therein lies the joy of life.

Undoubtedly, many people do act as though they believed it to be true, and a great many more, who would be dreadfully shocked if brought face to face with that proposition in cold blood, have, nevertheless, a vague feeling that such must be very much the way things are, even though they, themselves, are personally above consciously acting in accordance with such a notion. Now this is the real basis of sin, of resentment, of condemnation, of jealousy, of remorse, and all the evil brood that walk that path.

This belief in independent and separate existence is the arch sin, and now, before we can progress any further, we have to take the knife to this evil thing and cut it out once and for all. Jesus knew this, and with this definite end in view he inserted at this critical point a carefully prepared statement that would compass our end and his, without the shadow of a possibility of miscarrying. He inserted what is nothing less than a trip clause. He drafted a declaration which would force us, without any conceivable possibility of escape, evasion, mental reservation, or subterfuge of any kind, to execute the great sacrament of forgiveness in all its fullness and far-reaching power.

As we repeat the Great Prayer intelligently, considering and meaning what we say, we are suddenly, so to speak, caught up off our feet and grasped as though in a vise, so that we must face this problem – and there is no escape. We must positively and definitely extend forgiveness to everyone to whom it is possible that we can owe forgiveness, namely, to anyone who we think can have injured us in any way. Jesus leaves no room for any possible glossing of this fundamental thing. He has constructed his Prayer with more skill than ever yet lawyer displayed in the casting of a deed. He has so contrived it that once our attention has been drawn to this matter, we are inevitably obliged either to forgive our enemies in sincerity and truth, or never again to repeat that prayer. It is safe to say that no one who reads this booklet with understanding will ever again be able to use the Lord's Prayer unless and until he has forgiven. Should you now attempt to repeat it without forgiving, it can safely be predicted that you will not be able to finish it This great central clause will stick in your throat

Notice that Jesus does not say, "forgive me my trespasses and I will try to forgive others," or "I will see if it can be done," or "I will forgive generally, with certain exceptions." He obliges us to declare that we have actually forgiven, and forgiven all, and he makes our claim to our own forgiveness to depend upon that. Who is there who has grace enough to say his prayers at all, who does not long for the forgiveness or cancellation of his own mistakes and faults. Who would be so insane as to endeavor to seek the Kingdom of God without desiring to be relieved of his own sense of guilt. No one, we may believe. And so we see that we are trapped in the inescapable position that we cannot demand our own release before we have released our brother.

The forgiveness of others is the vestibule of Heaven, and Jesus knew it, and has led us to the door. You must forgive everyone who has ever hurt you if you want to be forgiven yourself; that is the long and the short of it. You have to get rid of all resentment and condemnation of others, and, not least, of self-condemnation and remorse. You have to forgive others, and having discontinued your own mistakes, you have to accept the forgiveness of God for them too, or you cannot make any progress. You have to forgive yourself, but you cannot forgive yourself sincerely until you have forgiven others first. Having forgiven others, you must be prepared to forgive yourself too, for to refuse to forgive oneself is only spiritual pride. "*And by that sin fell the angels.*" We cannot make this point too clear to ourselves; we have got to forgive. There are few people in the world who have not at some time or other been hurt, really hurt, by someone else; or been disappointed, or injured, or deceived, or misled. Such things sink into the memory where they usually cause inflamed and festering wounds, and there is only one remedy – they have to be plucked out and thrown away. And the one and only way to do that is by forgiveness.

Of course, nothing in all the world is easier than to forgive people who have not hurt us very much. Nothing is easier than to rise above the thought of a trifling loss. Anybody will be willing to do this, but what the Law of Being requires of us is that we forgive not only these trifles, but the very things that are so hard to forgive that at first it seems impossible to do it at all. The despairing heart cries, "It is too much to ask. That thing meant too much to me. It is impossible. I cannot forgive it." But the Lord's Prayer makes our own forgiveness from God, which means our escape from guilt and limitation, dependent upon just this very thing. There is no escape from this, and so forgiveness there must be, no matter how deeply we may have been injured, or how terribly we have suffered. It must be done.

If your prayers are not being answered, search your consciousness and see if there is not someone whom you have yet to forgive. Find out if there is not some old thing about which you are very resentful. Search and see if you are not really holding a grudge (it may be camouflaged in some self-righteous way) against some individual, or somebody of people, a nation, a race, a social class, some religious movement of which you disapprove perhaps, a political party, or what-not. If you are doing so, then you have an act of forgiveness to perform, and when this is done, you will probably make your demonstration. If you cannot forgive at present, you will have to wait for your demonstration until you can, and you will have to postpone finishing your recital of the Lord's Prayer too, or involve yourself in the position that you do not desire the forgiveness of God.

Setting others free means setting yourself free, because resentment is really a form of attachment. It is a Cosmic Truth that it takes two to make a prisoner; the prisoner— and a jailer. There is no such thing as being a prisoner on one's own account. Every prisoner must have a jailer, and the jailer is as much a prisoner as his charge. When you hold resentment against anyone, you are bound to that person by a cosmic link, a real, though mental chain. You are tied by a cosmic tie to the thing that you hate. The one person perhaps in the whole world whom you most dislike is the very one to whom you are attaching yourself by a hook that is stronger than steel. Is this what you wish? Is this the condition in which you desire to go on living? Remember, you belong to the thing with which you are linked in thought, and at some time or other, if that tie endures, the object of your resentment will be drawn again into your life, perhaps to work further havoc. Do you think that you can afford this? Of course, no one can afford such a thing; and so the way is clear. You must cut all such ties, by a clear and spiritual act of forgiveness. You must loose him and let him go. By forgiveness you set yourself free; you save your soul. And because the law of love works alike for one and all, you help to save his soul too, making it just so much easier for him to become what he ought to be.

But how, in the name of all that is wise and good, is the magic act of forgiveness to be accomplished, when we have been so deeply injured that, though we have long wished with all our hearts that we could forgive, we have nevertheless found it impossible; when we have tried and tried to forgive, but have found the task beyond us.

The technique of forgiveness is simple enough, and not very difficult to manage when you understand how. The only thing that is essential is willingness to forgive. Provided you desire to forgive the offender, the greater part of the work is already done. People have always made such a bogey of forgiveness because they have been under the erroneous impression that to forgive a person means that you have to compel yourself to like him. Happily, this is by no means the case – we are not called upon to like anyone whom we do not find ourselves liking spontaneously, and, indeed it is quite impossible to like people to order. You can no more like to order than you can hold the winds in your fist, and if you endeavor to coerce yourself into doing so, you will finish by disliking or hating the offender more than ever. People used to think that when someone had hurt them very much, it was their duty, as good Christians, to pump up, as it were, a feeling of liking for him; and since such a thing is utterly impossible, they suffered a great deal of distress, and ended, necessarily, with failure, and a resulting sense of sinfulness. We are not obliged to like anyone; but we are under a binding obligation to love everyone, love, or charity as the Bible calls it, meaning a vivid sense of impersonal good will. This has nothing directly to do with the feelings, though it is always followed, sooner or later, by a wonderful feeling of peace and happiness.

The method of forgiving is this: Get by yourself and become quiet. Repeat any prayer or treatment that appeals to you, or read a chapter of the Bible. Then quietly say, "I fully and freely forgive X (mentioning the name of the offender); I loose him and let him go. I completely forgive the whole business in question. As far as I am concerned, it is finished forever. I cast the burden of resentment upon the Christ within me. He is free now, and I am free too. I wish him well in every phase of his life. That incident is finished. The Christ Truth has set us both free. I thank God." Then get up and go about your business. On no account repeat this act of forgiveness, because you have done it once and for all, and to do it a second time would be tacitly to repudiate your own work. Afterward, whenever the memory of the offender or the offense happens to come into your mind, bless the delinquent briefly and dismiss the thought. Do this, however many times the thought may come back. After a few days it will return less and less often, until you forget it altogether. Then, perhaps after an interval, shorter or longer, the old trouble may come back to memory once more, but you will find that now all bitterness and resentment have disappeared, and you are both free with the perfect freedom of the children of God. Your forgiveness is complete. You will experience a wonderful joy in the realization of the demonstration.

Everybody should practice general forgiveness every day as a matter of course. When you say your daily prayers, issue a general amnesty, forgiving everyone who may have injured you in any way, and on no account, particularize. Simply say: "I freely forgive everyone." Then in the course of the day, should the thought of grievance or resentment come up, bless the offender briefly and dismiss the thought.

The result of this policy will be that very soon you will find yourself cleared of all resentment and condemnation, and the effect upon your happiness, your bodily health, and your general life will be nothing less than revolutionary.

Treat *the* Treatment

Spiritual treatment is really knowing the Truth about a given condition. There appears to be something wrong – someone is sick, or there is inharmony, or perhaps lack – but instead of accepting this, you remind yourself of the Truth. This reminding oneself of the Truth is a very powerful treatment, because in this way we do not try to wrestle with the evil, but we know that it is not there. The truth about life is that all is perfect, utter, unchanging harmony, because God is the only Presence and the only Power. As a student of metaphysics, you know this, and often merely reminding yourself of it brings a quick and beautiful demonstration. Of course, there are, however, so-called chronic cases in which the student, despite all he can do, seems to make no progress. I have known some obstinate and long-standing difficulties to be overcome by the following method: Give one final and definite treatment for the difficulty in question by reminding yourself of the Spiritual Truth concerning it, and then do not treat about the problem again but treat the treatment whenever you feel inclined to. Do this by claiming that that treatment was a Divine activity and must be successful. Claim that God worked through you when you gave the treatment and that God's work must succeed. Insist that your treatment, being a Divine activity, cannot be hindered by seeming difficulties or material conditions. Give thanks for its perfect success and mean what you say. This is "treating the treatment," and you may do this as often as you like. It has none of the disadvantages that are apt to arise from treating the problem itself too often.

Treat the "Because" When you find yourself thinking that your Prayer cannot be answered for any reason whatever – treat that reason. When something says to you that you cannot demonstrate "because" – treat the because. When you think, I cannot demonstrate because I have not enough understanding – treat for understanding. When you think, I cannot treat because I have a Headache – treat the headache. When you think, I cannot demonstrate because I am full of doubts – treat the doubts. When you think I cannot demonstrate because it is now too late – treat against the time illusion. When you think, I cannot demonstrate in this part of the country – treat against the space illusion. When you think, I cannot demonstrate this thing because of my age – treat your age belief. When you think, I cannot demonstrate because someone else will hinder me – treat the belief in a power other than God. No matter what name the because may give itself, it is still your belief in limitation. Be loyal to God and know that He and He alone has all power. Treat the because.

True Prosperity

In the scriptural sense, 'prosperity' and 'prosper' signify a very great deal more than the acquirement of material possessions. They really mean success in prayer. From the point of view from the soul, success in prayer is the only kind of prosperity worth having; and if our prayers are successful, we shall naturally have all the material things that we need. A certain quantity of material goods is essential on this plane, of course, but material wealth is really the least important thing in life, and this the Bible implies by giving the word 'prosperous' its true meaning.

Blessed are the poor in spirit; for theirs is the kingdom of heaven. To be poor in spirit does not in the least mean the thing we call 'poor spirited' nowadays. To be poor in spirit means to have emptied yourself of all desire to exercise personal self-will, and, what is just as important, to have renounced all preconceived opinions in the wholehearted search for God. It means to be willing to set aside your present habits of thought, your present views and prejudices, your present way of life if necessary; to jettison, in fact, anything and everything that can stand in the way of your finding God. One of the saddest passages in all literature is the story of the Rich Young Man who missed one of the great opportunities of history, and 'turned away sorrowful because he had great possessions'.

This is really the story of mankind in general. We reject the salvation that Jesus offers us – our chance of finding God – because 'we have great possessions'; not in the least because we are very rich in terms of money, for indeed most people are not, but because we have great possessions in the way of preconceived ideas – confidence in our own judgement, and in the ideas with which we happen to be familiar; spiritual pride, born of academic distinction; sentimental or material attachment to institutions and organizations, habits of life that we have no desire to renounce; concern for human respect, or perhaps fear of public ridicule; or a vested interest in worldly honor and distinction. And these possessions keep us chained to the rock of suffering that is our exile from God.

The Rich Young Man is one of the most tragic figures in history; not because he happened to be wealthy, for wealth in itself is neither good nor bad, but because his heart was enslaved by that love of money which Paul tells us is the root of all evil

Why was not the Christ Message received with acclaim by the ecclesiastics of Jerusalem? Because they had great possessions – possessions of Rabbinical learning, possessions of public honor and importance, authoritative offices as the official teachers of religion – and these possessions they would have had to sacrifice in order to accept the spiritual teaching. The humble and unlearned folk who heard the Master gladly were happy in having no such possessions to tempt them away from the Truth.

Why was it in modern times when the same simple Christ Message of the immanence and availability of God, and of the Inner Light that burns forever in the soul of man, once more made its appearance in the world, it was again, for the most part, among the simple and unlettered that it was gladly received? Why was it not the Bishops, and Deans, and Moderators, and Ministers, and Presbyteries, who gave it to the world? Why was not Oxford, or Cambridge, or Harvard, or Heidelberg, the great broadcasting center for this most important of all knowledge?

And, again the answer is – because they had great possessions – great possessions of intellectual and spiritual pride, great possessions of self-satisfaction and cocksureness, great possessions of academic commitment, and of social prestige.

The poor in spirit suffer from none of these embarrassments, either because they never had them, or because they have risen above them on the tide of spiritual understanding. They have got rid of the love of money and property, of fear of public opinion, and of the disapproval of relatives or friends. They are no longer overawed by human authority, however august. They are no longer cocksure in their own opinions. They have come to see that their most cherished beliefs may have been and probably were mistaken, and that all their ideas and views of life may be false and in need of recasting. They are ready to start again at the very beginning and learn life anew."

The Golden Key *to* Prayer

I have compressed the following essay into a few paragraphs. Had it been possible I would have reduced it to as many lines. It is not intended to be an instructional treatise, but a practical recipe for getting out of trouble. Study and research are well in their own time and place, but no amount of either will get you out of a concrete difficulty. Nothing but practical work in your own consciousness will do that. The mistake made by many people, when things go wrong, is to skim through book after book, without getting anywhere. Read *The Golden Key*[8] several times. Do exactly what it says, and if you are persistent enough you will overcome any difficulty.

Prayer will enable you, sooner or later, to get yourself, or anyone else, out of any difficulty on the face of the earth. It is the Golden Key to harmony and happiness. To those who have no acquaintance with the mightiest power in existence, this may appear to be a rash claim, but it needs only a fair trial to prove that, without a shadow

---

[8] *The Golden Key and Twenty-Two Additional Essays* (Merchant Books ISBN 978-1603867061)

of doubt, it is a just one. You need take no one's word for it, and you should not. Simply try it for yourself, and see.

God is omnipotent, and man is His image and likeness, and has dominion over all things. This is the inspired teaching, and it is intended to be taken literally, at its face value. Man means every man, and so the ability to draw on this power is not the special prerogative of the mystic or the saint, as is so often supposed, or even of the highly trained practitioner. Whoever you are, wherever you may be, the Golden Key to harmony is in your hand now. This is because in scientific prayer it is God who works, and not you, and so your particular limitations or weaknesses are of no account in the process. You are only the channel through which the divine action takes place, and your treatment will really be just the getting of yourself out of the way. Beginners often get startling results at the first time of trying, for all that is absolutely essential is to have an open mind, and sufficient faith to try the experiment. Apart from that, you may hold any views on religion, or none.

As for the actual method of working, like all fundamental things, it is simplicity itself. All that you have to do is this: Stop thinking about the difficulty, whatever it is, and think about God instead. This is the complete rule, and if only you will do this, the trouble, whatever it is, will presently disappear. It makes no difference what kind of trouble it is. It may be a big thing or a little thing; it may concern health, finance, a lawsuit, a quarrel, an accident, or anything else conceivable; but whatever it is, just stop thinking about it, and think of God instead — that is all you have to do.

The thing could not be simpler, could it? God Himself could scarcely have made it simpler, and yet it never fails to work when given a fair trial.

Do not try to form a picture of God, which is impossible. Work by rehearsing anything or everything that you know about God. God is Wisdom, Truth, inconceivable Love. God is present everywhere; has infinite power; knows everything; and so on. It matters not how well you may think you understand these things; go over them repeatedly.

But you must stop thinking of the trouble, whatever it is. The rule is to think about God, and if you are thinking about your difficulty you are not thinking about God. To be continually glancing over your shoulder, as it were, in order to see how matters are progressing, is fatal, because that is thinking of the trouble, and you must think of God, and of nothing else. Your object is to drive the thought of the difficulty right out of your consciousness, for a few moments at least, substituting for it the thought of God. This is the crux of the whole thing. If you can become so absorbed in this consideration of the spiritual world that you really forget for a while all about the trouble concerning which you began to pray, you will presently find that you are safely and comfortably out of your difficulty — that your demonstration is made.

In order to "Golden Key" a troublesome person or a difficult situation, think, "Now I am going to 'Golden Key' John, or Mary, or that threatened danger"; then proceed to drive all thought of John, or Mary, or the danger right out of your mind, replacing it by the thought of God. By working in this way about a person, you are not seeking to influence his conduct in any way, except that you prevent him from injuring or annoying you, and you do him nothing but good. Thereafter he is certain to be in some degree a better, wiser, and more spiritual person, just because you have "Golden Keyed" him. A pending lawsuit or other difficulty would probably fade out harmlessly without coming to a crisis, justice being done to all parties concerned.

If you find that you can do this very quickly, you may repeat the operation several times a day with intervals between. Be sure, however, each time you have done it, that you drop all thought of the matter until the next time. This is important.

We have said that the Golden Key is simple, and so it is, but, of course, it is not always easy to turn. If you are very frightened or worried it may be difficult, at first, to get your thoughts away from material things. But by constantly repeating some statement of absolute Truth that appeals to you, such as There is no power but God, or I am the child of God, filled and surrounded by the perfect peace of God, or God is love, or God is guiding me now, or, perhaps best and simplest of all, just God is with me — however mechanical or dead it may seem at first — you will soon find that the treatment has begun to "take," and that your mind is clearing. Do not struggle violently; be quiet but insistent. Each time that you find your attention wandering, just switch it straight back to God.

Do not try to think out in advance what the solution of your difficulty will probably turn out to be. This is technically called "outlining," and will only delay the demonstration. Leave the question of ways and means strictly to God. You want to get out of your difficulty — that is sufficient. You do your half, and God will never fail to do His.

"*Whosoever shall call upon the name of the Lord shall be saved.*"

What Is Scientific Prayer?

Scientific prayer or spiritual treatment is really the lifting of your consciousness above the level where you have met your problem. If only you can rise high enough in thought, the problem will the solve itself. This is really the only problem you have – to raise in consciousness. The more "difficult," which means the more deeply rooted in your thoughts, is the problem concerned, the higher you will have to rise. What is called a small trouble, will yield to a slight raise in consciousness. What is called a serious difficulty, will require a relatively higher rise. What is called a terrible danger or hopeless problem, will require a considerable rise in consciousness to overcome it – but that is the only difference.

Do not waste time trying to straighten out your own or other people's problems by manipulating thought – that gets you nowhere – but raise your consciousness, and the action of God will do the rest.

Jesus healed sick people and reformed many sinners by raising his consciousness above the picture they presented. He controlled the wind and the waves in the same way. He raised the dead because he was able to get as high in consciousness as is necessary to do this.

To raise your consciousness, you must positively withdraw your attention from the picture for the time being (The Golden Key) and then concentrate gently upon spiritual truth. You may do this by reading the Bible or any spiritual book that appeals to you, by going over any hymn or poem that helps you in this way, or by the use of one or more affirmations, just as you like.

I know many people who have secured the necessary elevation of consciousness by browsing at random through the Bible. A man I know was saved in a terrible shipwreck by quickly reading the 91st psalm. Another man healed himself of a supposedly hopeless disease by working on the one affirmation, "God Is Love," until he was able to realize something of what that greatest of all statements must really mean.

If you work with affirmations, be careful not to get tense; but there is no reason why you should not employ all these methods in turn, and also any others that you can think of. Sometimes a talk with a spiritual person gives you just the lift that you need. It matters not how you rise so long as you do rise. "I bore you on eagles' wings, and brought you unto myself."

You Can Alter Your Life

There is no need to be unhappy. There is no need to be sad. There is no need to be disappointed, or oppressed, or aggrieved. There is no need for illness or failure or discouragement. There is no necessity for anything but success, good health, prosperity, and an abounding interest and joy in life.

That the lives of many people are full of dreary things is unfortunately only too true; but there is no necessity for them to be there. They are there only because their victims suppose them to be inevitable, not because they are so. As long as you accept a negative condition at its own valuation, so long will you remain in bondage to it; but you have only to assert your birthright as a free man or woman and you will be free.

Success and happiness are the natural condition of mankind. It is actually easier for us to demonstrate these things than the reverse. Bad habits of thinking and acting may obscure this fact for a time, just as a wrong way of walking or sitting, or holding a pen or a musical instrument may seem to be easier than the proper way, because we have accustomed ourselves to it; but the proper way is the easier nevertheless.

Unhappiness, frustration, poverty, loneliness are really bad habits that their victims have become accustomed to bear with more or less fortitude, believing that there is no way out, whereas there is a way; and that way is simply to acquire good habits of mind instead of bad ones – habits of working with the Law instead of against it.

You should never "put up" with anything. You should never be willing to accept less than Health, Harmony, and Happiness. These things are your Divine Right as the sons and daughters of God, and it is only a bad habit, unconscious, as a rule, that causes you to be satisfied with less. In the depths of his being man always feels intuitively that there is a way out of his difficulties if only he can find it, and his natural instincts all point in the same direction.

The infant, as yet uncontaminated by the defeatist suggestions of his elders, simply refuses to tolerate inharmony on any terms, and therefore he demonstrates over it. When he is hungry he tells the world with a confident insistence that commands attention, while many a sophisticated adult goes without. Does he find a pin sticking in some part of his anatomy? Not for him a sigh of resignation to the supposed "will of God" (it is really blasphemy to say that evil or suffering could ever be the will of God, All Good), or a whine about never having any luck, or a sigh that what cannot be cured must be endured. No, the defeatist view of life has not yet touched him; his instincts tell him that life and harmony are, inseparable. And sure enough, that pin is located and removed even if everything else has to come to a stop until it is done.

But "shades of the prison-house begin to close about the growing boy," and by the time he is old enough to think rationally the Race habit will have trained him to use his reason largely in the inverted way.

Refuse to tolerate anything less than harmony. You can have prosperity no matter what your present circumstances may be. You can have health and physical fitness. You can have a happy and joyous life. You can have a good home of your own. You can have congenial friends and comrades. You can have a full, free, joyous life, independent and untrammeled. You can become your own master or your own mistress. But to do this you must definitely seize the rudder of your own destiny and steer boldly and firmly for the port that you intend to make.

What are you doing about your future? Are you content to let things just drift along as they are, hoping, like Mr. Micawber, for something to "turn up"? If you are, be assured that there is no escape in that way. Nothing ever will turn up unless you exercise your Free Will and go out and turn it up for yourself by becoming acquainted with the Laws of Life, and applying them to your own individual conditions. That is the only way. Otherwise the years will pass all too swiftly, leaving you just where you are now, if not worse off, for there is no limit to the result of thought either for good or evil.

Man has dominion over all things when he knows the Law of Being, and obeys it. The Law gives you power to bring any condition into your life that is not harmful. The Law gives you power to overcome your own weaknesses and faults of character, no matter how often you may have failed in the past or how tenacious they may have seemed to be. The Law gives you power to attain prosperity and position without infringing the rights and opportunities of anyone else in the world. The Law gives you Freedom; freedom of soul, and body, and environment.

The law gives you Independence so that you can build your own life in your own way, in accordance with yow own ideas and ideals; and plan out your future along the lines that you yourself desire. If you do not know what you really want to make you happy, then the Law will tell you what you want, and get it for you too. And the Law rightly understood and applied will save you from the danger of what is called "outlining" with all its risks and limitations.

The Law will endow you with the gift of what is called Originality; Originality is the doing of things in a new way which is a better way, and different from anyone else's way.

CPSIA information can be obtained
at www.ICGtesting.com
Printed in the USA
BVHW071423040821
613449BV00004B/524

9 781603 867498